fleeting things

rachel h

Fleeting Things.

Copyright © 2020 Rachel H

ISBN: 978-0-646-82201-3

eBook ISBN: 978-0-6453272-2-9

Cover Designer – Matthew Huckel

Editor – Susan G Scott

This book is published independently under the imprint ALittlePoetic Publishing

For enquiries, visit rachelhuckel.com or email rachelhuckel@gmail.com

contents

there is a place between
hurt and healing, between
dreams and reality, between
beginnings and endings, between
head and heart.

this place is where we live.
this place is where i write.

the bravery in
trusting

beekeeper

my secrets don't rest
on the tip of my tongue,
they nest in the
pits of my stomach.

there is a swarm of bees
in my abdomen.

all sting.
no honey.

and i'm not sure i can
keep them much longer.

collision

i don't know what else to say
except that you loved me at full speed,
foot never leaving the accelerator
and honestly, i'm still trying to recover
from being the red light you ran,
and from the way your eyes
looked like a deer in the headlights
when you were the one
driving the car.

tear stains

when i woke up,
there were tear stains
on my pillow
and although
i don't remember them,
i knew you must have
visited my dreams.

you always come back to me.

like breathing in.
the rising of the tide.

i have tried to let you go but
you always come back to me.

like an inhale.
an incoming wave.

and i am left breathing water,
praying that next time
the air will taste like

something new.

i carry you

i carry you with me everywhere i go.
i carry the heavy weight of all my thoughts of you
in these bags underneath my eyes.
they remind me that
you are the reason for my insomnia.

bed sheets

some mornings,
these bed sheets
are the heaviest
things in the world.

careful

(a) you always made me cross the road before i was ready. you never looked both ways and i always wanted to double-check. you always said i cared too much. about you. about me. about everything. as though there was a standard amount to caring, like standard amounts of alcohol. as though caring too much equated to lost inhibitions and caring too little meant you were safe to drive. the irony being that we were not behind the wheel – we were pedestrians crossing at the wrong time. i was just trying to be careful.

(b) i still remember the way you dug your heels into the ground. the way you used to kick up dirt. (how you never let things settle.) i told you to be careful but you always said it was *just* earth. *just* me. but this planet and its people are not *just* anything.

(c) you always thought i cried too much. maybe i did; maybe i didn't. they say laughter is the best medicine but i've always thought crying was one too – a prescription labelled "use as much as needed". it was needed sometimes when i watched the news, but you never understood. they were *just* strangers to you. (but to me they were us as well.)

(d) i crossed the road today. only this time i waited for the lights to change. it took almost three minutes but i believe in patience. my time will come. and it did today. the entire intersection stopped (eight lanes of traffic) and i was the only one crossing. yes, *just* me and yes, *just* crossing the road but i finally felt free. like i had finally found a way to care without the shackles. like caring was taking me places. the right ones. at the right times.

(e) this is a poem addressed to you, that is not really for you. it is for me. a reminder to never stop being careful. with the world. with people. with myself. always take care. always care.

(f) always.

people think writers are stupid.
we choose to relive our heartache
on paper for the sake of art.

i think writers are strong.
we enter the most dangerous territories
of our minds and yet
we still don't break...

we make.

why did you become a writer? you ask.

what can i tell you? i can tell you how when i was little, i never wanted to play with others because they always ruined the plot i had imagined in my head. i can tell you how in school, words began appearing on my study notes during class. they crept onto serviettes at the dining table. climbed onto the backs of abandoned receipts when i worked at the checkout counter. i can tell you that my mind is always writing without me telling it to. it wasn't a choice. i am always sinking deeper and deeper into my own world. i can't help it. no one can hurt me there.

i can see people looking at me in these moments – when i have sunk into the depths of my own mind. i can hear muffled sounds saying that i look like i've seen a ghost. sometimes i feel like one. like everything just keeps slipping away and the only thing i've been able to hold onto is a pen. you ask me who i am and i say a writer but take away that title, and i am left with only poorly-timed daydreams and ink-stained fingers. i am caught between having my feet on the ground and my head in the clouds and writing is the place where they meet.

sometimes i feel like i will never be more than an abstract idea. like i am made up only of secrets and metaphors. will the essence of who i am always be this intangible? when my mind is far away, i don't stop to notice what i leave behind in reality. i know i am housed in this body but it has never really felt like a home. i have lived only half my life in it. the rest i have lived in my head.

i was once asked if i want to be loved and in all honesty, i've never given it much thought. i don't know why anyone would ever want to. i've spent my life running away from myself only to keep running into more of myself. is it a blessing or a curse to be a never-ending story that i could spend eternity trying to pen down?

the thing about love is, i've only ever wanted to give it out to everyone. but it feels a lot like standing on a street corner and giving out free samples, only to watch it all get discarded in the nearest bin. i've found that i can't give people the world because my world is rather different. all i can give you is my thoughts on paper. this is where i exist. here i am. leave if you like but i will continue to be. who i am.

why? you ask.

perhaps the answer is simple after all.
it is for the same reason i became a writer:

i simply cannot stop.

healing hurts

it's quite a paradox –
the way healing hurts.
memories are like saltwater
in my wounds –
a necessary sting.

when new skin grows, the memory
will of course still be a part of me.

i am simply washing off
the pain associated with it.

forgiveness

(1) when i was fifteen i first lost the ability to breathe. that was when i started counting. i counted sheep when i couldn't sleep at night. i counted the number of times i would hunch over the toilet bowl but could never get you to leave my system. they warn us about intoxication but never tell us that people can be a kind of poison.

(2) when i was sixteen i learned that the presence of one person can consume me. years later, i still taste campfires when i think of you – the anger has settled but i still cough up ashes and smoke. sometimes i hope i've started to forget you but these nights are all tainted with the times i'd see you out of the corner of my eye and silently struggle for breath. when you'd sit next to me around the campfire and all the singing in me stopped.

(3) when i was seventeen i read your letter. i told myself it changed nothing but i read it and cried. then read it and cried again. it's still sitting in my drawer – three folds and one objective. the paper holds the aftermath of all your decisions. you were never one to wear your words. that was always my job. sometimes i think i waited for an apology so long that i became one.

(4) i am eighteen and i am putting everything back in its place. i have stopped counting the years and the tears and i'm beginning to take the time back. i am working on forgiving you. i am working on

forgiving myself too. one day i will call you and tell you that your actions were never mine to carry. but i don't need you to take them back for me to start unloading them from my shoulders. i take responsibility for my hands but not yours. and the ability to breathe?

i finally take that back too.

the time my heart got its voice back

one time i woke and my eyelids weren't heavy
and sleep was just rest
and my dreams were even sweeter in the light.
the air was just air, not an ocean,
and my ankles were no longer anchored.
my arms were like feathers,
like the freedom that comes with flying
and i moved them in melodies that
sounded like my own.

i had been waiting for such soft songs of victory.
my anatomy was its own orchestra.
i wriggled my toes like piano keys,
listened to my heart beat like a drum,
let my hair sway gently like a harp.

i rose rhythmically into grace,
stepped slowly into healing.
and i allowed my heart to sing
for as long and as loudly
as it wanted to. because oh,
there were so many times when it could not.

changing directions

i have watched so many rotations of clock hands and endless calendar pages flip. i'm a hopeless believer in fresh starts, but time doesn't change very much – people do. i used to believe moving on meant moving forward, but now i think it means changing directions.

growth

growth is a wildly misunderstood notion. sometimes it's about moving backwards instead of forward. autumn itself teaches us that loss, in time, has purpose. leaves fall and break down; so too is it inevitable that people break down and tears fall. what you don't see is how your tears just might become water for those struggling to sprout, and how your broken pieces just might scatter as seeds of hope.

you might not grow in the way you expected, but being part of the lives that bloom around you is an experience far more incredible.

trust

(1) we seem to be on a quest for it. like it is a tangible item buried somewhere in the woods for us to find. but am i the hunter or am i the prey? we look for it as an answer, but all i've found are questions.

(2) why is it always misplaced? i concealed it above rabbit holes, left it to capture those who were just trying to get closer to me. is my guard actually down if i hurt others before they hurt me, or am i just using an attack as a defence?

(3) do you trust me not to hurt you? it always seems to be the unasked question in the hesitation between exchanges of secrets. if i pull you out of the rabbit holes i let you fall down, would i be earning your trust or losing it?

trust fall

i was taught to test the waters
instead of taking a leap of faith.
right from when i was a child
i learnt this was a way to keep me safe.

i was taught to test the waters
instead of diving in too deep
so i learnt to do this with people
before i gave them secrets to keep.

i was taught that trust needs to be earnt
instead of being given from the start
so i dip my toes in promises,
being oh so careful with my heart.

but i'm afraid i'm overflowing
with all the things i keep locked inside
and your depths look like the safest place
for my heart's secrets to hide.

there is no time to test the waters;
i'm jumping headfirst, falling down.
and if i break as i hit the water,
just please don't let me drown.

she had a library

she had a library, you see,
with many different stories to loan.
but the ones you couldn't borrow
were those that were her own.

they sat there on the bookshelf,
abandoned, collecting dust,
for those she used to show them to
had all broken her trust.

there were some chapters
that to them looked out of place,
and even some words
that they had tried to erase.

there were some empty shelves
because of all the stories they took
and other shelves full of tales
that had never been given a look.

one day a boy came in
and began to fill his cart
with all the books
she'd written from her heart.

at first, she was terrified
but he promised to stay
and read every single one
without stopping halfway.

he brushed off the dust
from the stories that were forgotten
and worked through the pile
until he finally reached the bottom.

then through the stacks of books
he began to try to weave –
you can imagine her heartbreak
when he got up to leave.

but he grabbed her hand
and led her through the door,
for this was just one library
and there were many more.

he told her that he loved
every single word he read,
and he wasn't forgetting her library
but showing her his instead.

he wasn't one metaphor

sometimes he was deep;
sometimes he was shallow,
from different facades he'd leap.

you could search a landscape
but you would never find
a single piece of nature
where he could be defined.

i guess he was a rock –
proud and confident, he stayed.
but he was also a tree –
under the weight of doubt, he swayed.

i think he was the sky –
there wasn't much he concealed.
but he was also the ocean –
a world waiting to be revealed.

he wasn't black and white,
but neither was he grey.
he was a whole realm of colours
all which he held within a day.

i have a habit of wondering,
a longing to know each thought,
but somehow for him i never
found the answer that i sought.

and yet i know i don't have
a right to be in someone's head,
i must respect that i'll never know
the things he hasn't said.

i have no expectations
for what i would find in there.
whether thoughts beautiful or ugly,
i'd most certainly still care.

i think it's just not knowing
that frustrates me the most.
no matter how hard i try,
i never even come close.

tell me again

tell me again about the chaos
exploding beneath your skin

because i know i don't see it

but every untidy piece of you
(those that you sweep into corners
and push into closets) –

i want to hold those too.

closed doors

i remember the times i visited your mind,
i walked inside but didn't get very far.
you have put up so many roadblocks
to stop people from knowing who you are.

but there are parts you've told me before,
please don't think i'll ever forget.
i may forget your birthday or number of siblings
but i'll remember what makes you happy and upset.

they say a man's mind has many rooms
and you've said there's a locked one for me.
you've told me some of what's beyond the door
but i'd much rather you gave me the key.

i guess you aren't the only one who hides things –
there is so much about you i've left unsaid.
but you don't understand the gnawing frustration
of wanting to know all the thoughts in your head.

i know you have many shadowed thoughts
(i've walked the beginning of that track).
but i want to know your darkest thoughts too –
i'm not afraid to walk in the pitch black.

i think the path you try the hardest to conceal
leads to the most beautiful part of your mind.
it's wild and messy and dangerous
and best of all, it's purely unrefined.

i've known you for quite some time now,
we've confided secrets that no one else knows.
and we know we can trust each other,
yet there are many doors that we've kept closed.

you can't comprehend how much i care for you –
so much that it's agonising when we speak.
we've spent hours at the entrance of your mind
but beyond that you've only let me peek.

you and the chaos

you and the chaos you carry.
a hurricane on two legs.
the finality of the thunder.
the bitter cry of the rain.
nothing hits the ground without an echo.
no disaster walks away unscathed.
even if it is a scrape of a knee,
a slightly tattered heart:
i want you to know that i see you.

i want you to know that
i am not afraid of your storms.

the accident

you picked me up at five-pm
when a purpose-driven city
made its way home.
but we were driving aimlessly
just so we could be alone.

it felt like we were going
so much faster than we were.
but half-asleep
in your passenger seat was when
the lines all started to blur.

the reflection of red lights
bounced off your rear-view mirror
but you didn't look back.
five-pm bled into two-am
and purple bled into black.

then you were so distracted
telling your story that
you missed a speed bump,
scraped the bottom of your
third-hand car.

i can't stop my mind
running over that moment –
a few near misses
before the accident
of getting to know who you are.

some kind of alchemist

i had not met a person
who had the power to turn everything
they touched to gold.

i had once believed this to be
the definition of magic –
i thought that their touch
must have to make things more beautiful.

but i had instead met a person
who had a kind of magic
that they were unaware of.

for it was not the things they touched
that were made beautiful –
there were places they had not been,
songs they had not heard.

but to me, these places and songs
were explosions of colours,
reflecting hues of hope
like a rainbow after a storm.

i had not found the pot of the gold at the end.
but i no longer searched for gold –

i had already found beauty everywhere,
simply because they touched my heart
and left a part of their magic behind.

don't leave just yet

i wish i could sit with you
and show you the beauty of this world
despite its mess.
we could watch the falling leaves
and i could explain
how they are a metaphor for
hope,
renewal,
restoration.
i could trace the edges of the leaf,
trace the clouds in the sky.
but what i really wish i could do
is trace your hand
and show you your beauty
despite your mess.
show you that you too
can be a symbol for
hope,
renewal,
restoration.
don't leave just yet.
it might be chaos
but there is harmony in nature
and i believe that one day
you will find it in yourself.

a love that just was

you and i had a love
like the trees and the rain –
a love that just was
and will never come again.

i was ever flowing through you
because you needed me to thrive –
falling over and over
just to keep you alive.

no matter the forecast

some days i am the clouds of whipped frosting
and on the sunny days like these
you promise me you'll admire me
like someone gazing at the sky in wonder.
you promise me you'll explore me
and find peace in all that i am and all that i can be.

some days i am the clouds made of nothing but rain
and on the stormy days like these
you promise me you'll never run for shelter
even when i am as grey as the gravel
on an abandoned road,
heavy and weighed down
by the fluid of my mind.
you promise me you'll keep me safe
in times when i'm terrified of my own darkness.

but would you promise to stay
even if it meant more shadows than light?
are you willing to be exposed
to the weather my heart creates?

because there is more to this than meteorology.

oh, when the rain hits the ground,
know that i'm falling for you so much harder.
the weather is unpredictable,
but the love i have for you will endure.
and i promise

i will always keep you in the eye of my storm.

tiny vault

he gave her a shell
when she felt the furthest from free,
hoping she would put it to her ear
and remember the sea.

she heard the whisper of the wind
as it carried secrets across the shore
and was reminded of the times
she had been there before:

when she had stood before the waves
with many things to hide
and allowed her troubles to be trapped
beneath the mysterious tide.

the rhythms of the ocean
always brought a peace to her soul
and lent her its power to be wild
but also in control.

it was never gold or silver
that she held in her treasury,
but the blissful melodies of the shell –
a tiny vault of a memory.

if only wings worked in water

i am a butterfly taught to love the sky
but i fell deeply in love with the sea.
i'm afraid i can only fly away or drown –
this is a love that is never meant to be.

i'm still praying for my
wings to work in water.

(and i'm still praying
for you and me.)

magicians

i always believed that you were magic.
i just never expected your final disappearing act.

wrecked things

i am not good at caring for the things i love.
i don't keep them in glass cabinets,
i carry them with me.

too many books i have dog-eared the pages of.
i have underlined sentences,
scribbled notes,
spilled coffee.

i make it so it is impossible
for me to return them. and though
they are wrecked things,
they are unmistakeably mine.

i just hope that one day

i will be the messy thing
somebody wants to hold on to.

i am tired of
falling in love
with wings.

fragments.

fleeting things.

unsaid goodbyes

the sun is setting and i can't see it because the clouds
are in the way. but that's okay. you've already shown
me the fear of when something beautiful disappears.
without a goodbye, without knowing why. i try to see
through – to the sun, to you. but you're clouded with
pride. you hide until you fade from view. it's true that
goodbyes are painful. but now you must explain to my
heart why you had to depart and take away your
warmth and your light. i fight the darkness every night,
and i wish i was brave, but i am afraid that the sun will
never rise. it wasn't wise to give you so much power
over me. you see, now there's not enough left to
generate electricity. and i'm scared and stumbling in
the cold but i'm told that my body will adjust. it must.
it's just learnt not to trust.

sometimes the lonely moonlight hour
rears its ugly head and
i write you letters from a heart
that is too empty to say anything,
other than to tell you that

at least one of us is wanted.

walking you home

a secret?
i miss you the most when it rains.
it reminds me of the spotted umbrella i used to carry everywhere. how when it started to rain you would run up behind me like a bird seeking shelter. and how i would tip the umbrella your way – make room for you in more ways than one.

a secret?
i scarcely carry an umbrella these days.
most of the time, i'm too tired to run for cover, too tired to keep missing you like i do. when it rains i always lose my balance – always trip up somewhere down memory lane. and my heart ends up soaking like wet socks from a puddle i didn't see coming.

a secret?
i saw you coming.
i just wanted another excuse to walk you home.

would it be selfish to ask you
not to forget me?

you can decide whether it's
the good or bad.

after all we've been through,
i would just like to have left
a trace of me behind.

keep a fragmented
version of me
in your mind
like

        the smell of rain that

           lingers

after it has
ceased to

fall.

i need to know that
throughout this huge earth,
a part of me will always have

a home with you.

small cases of déjà vu

i have let you go a thousand times over.

but there is still my heart and
its small cases of déjà vu:

when the clouds cover the sunlight,
when the shadows sweep goosebumps
across my skin

and for a fleeting moment,
my heart remembers a feeling.

just a flicker.
just a brief second of longing.

but then the sunlight
comes back out

and the moment passes

and i have to let go of you
again.

learning

i know (i know)
everything (everyone)
is a lesson.

but sometimes i wish
i could stop learning
and just start living.

lost things and where to find them

i think i've lost my mind
and i was always taught that
when you lose things,
you should go back to where
you last had them.

that's where i keep running into you.

you don't just let go once

you let go when you decide to turn on the lights as you wake up, instead of lying in the dark and missing them.

you let go when you decide to turn on the news as you drink your coffee, instead of staring out the window and missing them.

you let go when you decide to turn on the radio as you shower, instead of drowning yourself in thoughts and missing them.

i let you go a thousand times over before i even left the house this morning and i will keep trying to let you go for as long as it takes to stop missing you.

physics

i used to miss you over cups of coffee.

(1) the bittersweet taste of a new beginning. thoughts of you never sat still, never fit between the lines like they do now. if they had, maybe i would have been able to read the truth – that a bittersweet feeling has only ever clung to moments like trading in VCR players and graduating high school and other things soon to be past tense.

(2) the rush between sips. the anticipation. the buzz of electricity that looks like airport departure boards and feels like taking off. i used to think you brought the world to my fingertips, but i think i just made my world smaller. until it only looked like you.

(3) the moment of suspension. or some other type of physics i could never quite wrap my head around. i trusted you like a one-way ticket to happiness and you left me thousands of feet high. if i had given a thought to what physics and all those cups of coffee had taught me, i would have known that sooner or later with you, it would all come crashing down.

tender

in my dreams, you are nothing but tender.
you are the person who reaches out a hand
to help me get over big puddles,
that hauls my heavy luggage onto the bus.

only i don't tell you that you are what
i am trying to get over –
that you are the heavy thing i am carrying.

badge of honour

maybe one day i'll wear what happened
like a badge of honour, instead of
hiding it in shame. i'll say,
'look. i cared. i loved. and i am proud',
and what became of that
will no longer matter.

stranger on the early morning train

there is a stranger on the train
who reminds me too much of you.
it is still the early morning;
there is still so much to do.

we don't have much in common
except a shared awe for the storm,
yet it morphs into conversation –
both phenomena out of the norm.

so we talk but i don't tell them
about this sense of déjà vu.
they will never know they remind me
of someone i once knew.

we are headed different places
but for a moment we share the same time,
like that short but sacred feeling
of being yours, of you being mine.

i think that's what i miss the most:
just the time we spent alone,
knowing i have memories of you
that are completely my own.

is this what losing you has come to?
is this the eighth stage of grief?
finding you in exchanges
destined only to be brief?

i wish i could stay on this train longer.
there's still so much i don't understand.
but instead i say goodbye
and i shake the stranger's hand.

i am grateful that i met them;
i am grateful i met you.
but it is still the early morning;
there is still so much to do.

decisions

i used to believe that decisions
were either right or wrong,
that we were meant to travel roads
where our journey would be long.

but lately i've been thinking
some paths are for short seasons
and moving on doesn't mean
that we had the wrong reasons.

if dreams don't make sense any more,
is it wrong to say goodbye?
and if lovers end up parting ways,
does it mean they were wrong to try?

maybe we are too hard on ourselves
when we come to a fork in the road.
and i think it's time that we stopped
carrying our mistakes as a heavy load.

you will always wear your decisions,
but it is you who chooses how.
so wear your past with pride because
it's brought you to where you are now.

scattered

i need you to know
that the words don't pour out.
not like they used to.
they still come.
but they come on a tuesday morning
or a rainy afternoon.
scattered.

i suppose i am telling you this
because i need you to know
that missing you did more for me
than being with you ever could.
i wrung my heart out
just to romanticise
whatever it was i was drowning in.

words are a natural phenomenon.
they will come and go
like flood season and drought.
i know.

i'm just writing this
because i really need you to know
that when they return
you don't get to come with them.

how to tell you are healing

(1) if you think about who/what hurt you less. maybe you went thirty seconds without thinking about it. if that's an improvement then be proud of it.

(2) if you smile more. not at funny things but at little things like the warmth that spreads from your fingertips when you are holding a hot drink. life hurts but life is also so beautiful.

(3) if you feel a passion returning. maybe you didn't play the piano today but maybe your hands danced on the tabletop. you might not be ready to chase your dreams but be excited if you remember them.

(4) if you are still breathing. with each breath, time does more than you know. if you're living, then you are healing ever so slowly, but still healing, nonetheless. be patient with the process.

the art in attachment

there is a certain art in attachment.

when you reach out into this extraordinary world,
you will grow to love things and
they will become part of you. at first,
you will nurture people and dreams with open arms.

you will stretch your branches to make room for
them, strengthen your roots to keep them safe,
share your energy to help them thrive.

but in time, the seasons will change.
the things you love will start bursting at the seams
with new colours and there will come a time when
you need to let them go.

there is a certain art to this too.

trust that things are not falling apart,
they are falling perfectly into place.

can't you see how hurt becomes joy?
underneath your branches, a child tosses
richly-coloured leaves into the air like confetti.
i want to join her in celebration of all the things
that have come and gone
to make you exactly who you are.

you are part of this intrinsic pattern of creation.
don't you think it's beautiful?
you have loved and lost, and you are still remaining.
don't you think it makes you brave?

peter pan

you try hard to catch your shadow
but it moves much too fast.
it jumps on the walls and ceilings,
begging you to revisit your past.

nostalgia is a powerful state
and your memories give you flight.
you remember the instructions –
"second star to the right…"

here nothing is lost,
you still have every single friend
and on the morning horizon,
you see your innocence suspend.

but oh, remember now
you have far different dreams
and it's okay for life to not be the same
because we're growing up, it seems.

i hope your life is still an adventure –
one that's wild and grand.
but i think it's time to live it here,
i think it's time to leave Neverland.

crossword puzzles

i don't know exactly in which breath i broke and in which breath i healed. it's all a blur of slow fades and quick unravellings, gradual growth and sudden revelations. seasons of life overlapped like crossword puzzles, except i had no clues to solve the problems. reality was not quite as black and white but i got here, didn't i? the pen markings are evidence that life is just one big mess of trial and error. i think in a way i am still breaking and still healing and my heart is still working overtime to keep me safe. once it starts it does not stop but, my word, i do not want it to. see how i am a little less scared and a little bit stronger and oh, see how i'm doing just fine.

in spite of it all

i would still tell my past self
to love as hard as she did
and i will tell my future self
to love even harder.

the fight behind
staying

green lights

i stop at green lights.
to me, that is anxiety.

bad habits

sometimes i think i have a tighter grip on the bad than the good. habits are no exception to this. what is it about humans that makes us want to hurt ourselves? i used to hate looking in the mirror, but i only stared longer. many times, i spent so long fixating on those who hurt me that i almost forgot about the ones who didn't. i noticed i began to bite my lip when i was nervous but i only thought more. bit harder.

as i got older, i learnt too much about how to make my heart hurt. i could write my way out of breakdowns but more often than not, i wrote myself into them. but i did not mind. i, with my unfortunate habit of turning people into poetry, opened wounds for words. in a way, i did not want to heal.

i don't think i've ever been much good at holding on to happiness. in the mirror, i catch myself smiling but shy away. i think about people who make my heart light and something in me wants to run away and hide.

i've never been much good at fixing my bad habits but i would like to be better. because maybe if i learn to keep good habits, i can learn to keep good people too. maybe then i will have the courage to open new doors, but more importantly, have the courage to leave the old ones closed. maybe then i can loosen my grip on the bad: let it come but not let it stay. maybe then i can write about what i feel, not what i felt.

and yes, maybe i will try for hours to put pen to paper and come away with nothing but paper cuts. but thank goodness that for once, it'll only be my hands that hurt.

searching

a strange thing,
happiness.

all the places we search for it.

all the ways we try to hold it
between our teeth.
(the bottom lip of a stranger.)
(a fresh cup of coffee.)

things that will lose their heat
after a moment has passed.

and yet,
this does not stop us
from trying to fill the gaps
in our smiles
with something temporary.

it does not stop
the dull toothache.
(even our bones know
we were made for
better things.)

a strange thing,
happiness.

we are only searching for it
as a means of survival.

and if we stopped, we'd have
to admit that it is living
we are looking for.

so we don't stop,
because we are still
scraping by,
and strangely,
we think it is easier
than letting go.

belonging

sometimes i feel like i am simply being
passed into different hands.

we make homes out of people,
only to pack up our things
and move
and move
and move.

there is a lot of myself
still residing in cardboard boxes.
i am too scared to find a place for it.

i hover at your doorstep.
you look like exactly where i need to be
right now. but i've got a pocket full of old keys
to remind me to never overstay my welcome.

invite me in anyway.
there is something about you that
makes me want more than anything
to give all this another try.

ultimately

i just want to be with someone
who makes
adventures out of missed buses,
laughter out of forgotten umbrellas
and art out of all my mess.

i don't know much about
how to label the things i feel.

all i know is that
when i look at the sky,
i see freedom.

when i look at the dirt,
i see breakthrough.

when i look at the ocean,
i see serenity.

and when i look at you,

i see everything.

you are

the post-it note reminder.
the announcement on the train.
the banner in the sky.
the thought that attracts my attention,
screaming in a soft whisper:

better things are coming.

but you don't know that they are already here.
you don't know that you are all of them.

waves

there are oceans
in your eyes, and
when i see them,
feelings hit me
like waves.

patterns

memories follow such odd patterns. i don't remember
what i had for dinner last night, but i remember sitting
in my first-grade classroom, listening to my grey-haired
teacher talk about flames.

'be careful,' she said, 'they look pretty when they
flicker but they can easily become a fire'.

years have passed since then, but it's a lesson that has
never left me. it comes back in the form of a perfectly
timed raindrop that rolls lazily down my spine just
seconds before the sound of thunder.

years have passed and this pattern has somehow found
its way to people too. my eyes drowsily trace around
his fingertips and suddenly i am that same little girl
sitting cross-legged on the classroom floor wondering,

will things always be most beautiful right before they destroy you?

happiness is

a tear in the fabric.
a washed-out colour.
and i'm afraid to wear it
because
feelings fade
feelings fade
feelings fade.

listen

we can call it things like
patience.
caution.
timing.

we can call it anything we want to really.

but listen:
we let the storm clouds
dictate our movements
before a single raindrop has fallen

and oh, how much time we are wasting.

cold hands

if i wrote you a letter,
would you read between the lines?
i know i am scared
but i don't know what this defines.
you've got these cold hands
and i've got cold feet.
i'm worried if we're too parallel
that we will never meet.
do we get a say
in who our hands want to hold?
i pushed you out the door,
now the morning sun is cold.
you were always the sunrise.
i could not say it better.
(not even between the lines.
not even in a letter.)

i bolted the door
to keep my feet dry.
i wrote down all the reasons
but choked on the goodbye.
there is living and <u>loving</u>.
(i underlined the latter.)
i'm not good at either
but what does it matter?
my lungs still want air.
my heart still wants you.
so maybe i'm not good at them
but they are all i know how to do.
if i gave you this letter,
would you read between the lines?
your light still finds me
through closed doors and blinds.

the storm

there is pain here and they tell us not to touch it.

but either way, we feel it.
it festers behind the clouds.
builds. shakes the ground.

oh, we are well-versed in thunder.
by now we know lightning by name.
but we still do not touch it.
we still do as we're told.

hear me out: what if we weren't afraid?
we flee at the sight of rain but what if we
huddled closer? pressed ourselves tighter?
didn't allow it to part us?

i would whisper you this secret:
the sun has never healed us quite like the storm.

when shy hands hold

the truth is, i have no idea what i am doing.
in all honesty, it might just end terribly
but oh, it is beginning wonderfully and for now,
just hold my hand and let that be enough.

january

i kissed you and january
fell out of your mouth:
a string of resolutions
you were planning to break
and oh, how i hoped
my heart wasn't one of them.

warning sign

to be human is to know of warning signs:
what they mean & how to recognise them.
(the sky clouding over.)
(the stovetop heating up.)

we are standing in the kitchen.
the heat from the saucepan
fogs up the window.
obscures my view.
i can't see the sky but
truthfully, even if it is blue today,
it might not be tomorrow.

even if we while away the afternoon
in this safe place we've built together,

i still know you as a warning sign.
(i don't know how to see you as anything else.)

unravelling

sometimes i feel like the anxiety is a corset fastened
around my ribcage and i am nothing more than an
exhale away from unravelling. i haven't figured out
how to stop wearing my thoughts – how to keep them
from digging into me under my clothes. lately it seems
like this is all i do. i take unconscious worries and
unlikely truths and wrap myself up in them. tighter &
tighter & tighter. still, my mind does not stop pulling
at loose threads. or perhaps i am simply trying to hold
on to something certain. something i can use to retrace
my steps in the inevitable case that i get lost in
thoughts i have not yet proven to be true. this is why
i'm afraid to start the day. i'm afraid that i will lose
(myself). so i take a deep breath and begin. but
sometimes i feel like i am nothing more than an exhale
away from unravelling.

i will find you. i will find you curled up in corners, reading by candle flame, holding your breath just a little longer than you should. i will find you in rainstorms as you stand still, clutching your umbrella with both hands as it pours. i will find you walking through the streets at the break of dawn, rushing even though you have no place to be. i will find you, i whisper to my lost and troubled soul.

i will find you.

desperate

there are poems
beneath your skin
that are
desperate for air.

(the letters latch on
to your exhales
and i do my best
to catch them
on the way out.)

infinite

one. it's just a number, isn't it? just like two and three and four. it is nothing to be afraid of. and yet, i am terrified of firsts. because when i think of the first time i stumbled on feelings for you, i can recall how you were standing and how an involuntary flip in my abdomen turned all my words to scrambled letters. i think of the first time you held my hand and i can feel sand between my toes. we left footprints in more than one place that day. there are imprints of all these beginnings in my mind like lovers who etch their initials into wet concrete. and i'm worried that i'm going to write it all wrong. more than that, i am afraid to run out of firsts. one is a finite number. we can count to mississippi as many times as we like but eventually the second will end, won't it? in high school, i learned to count to ten in italian but i'm not sure what language we speak between one another. i'm not sure how high we can count. one. a stomach flip. two. a nervous hand. three. an overdue kiss. but i am trying to stop counting the moments. i am trying to stop unscrambling the letters. i think we are stuck somewhere in the drying cement. caught somewhere between one and infinite. we've got nothing but time.

you are my daydreams

you see, i've been thinking
about us so much, i almost
forgot the sound of
my own voice. but oh,
how i remember yours.

before 5am

just like morning, you arrive before the light does. it's 4:32am and you're parked outside of my house. it feels different meeting you at this time. it feels like we are two teenagers running away, and perhaps, in a way, we are. 'good morning.' 'is it?' i open the door to your sleepy silhouette cooped up in front of the driving wheel. i am still struggling to understand how you are a gentle hum, the dim comfort of a familiar face, but also a loud crashing sound, a breaking wave of electricity long before we've even reached the ocean. we are headed for the coastline to watch the sunrise but i don't know how to tell you that when you smile, i've already seen it. that in every poem i've tried to write about you, i always do full circles back to the same metaphor. always come to similar conclusions that i'm terrified to admit. but in this odd kind of darkness, it's as plain as day. the truth is not hidden in poems and riddles and metaphors. the truth is your morning voice – the coarse, rhythmic sound like water hitting rocks that sends my mind tumbling into an endless sea of things i'm not quite sure how to tell you. right now though, one thought continues to resurface. right now, i think i really might be starting to love you. all after good morning. all before 5am.

no other choice

you don't give me permission
to be who i am;
you give me no other choice.

i'm trying to fight the urge
to spill out all that is in me but
you make it so difficult.

you've got me thinking
that this is a good idea –
that maybe, just maybe,
who i am might be
a good thing after all.

i had only ever hoped
to find someone to
forgive my flaws but

you make me forget them.

white space

you are the white space in a poem.

a pause for reflection.

breathing room.

(everything i do not know how to say.)

oxygen

you came into my life
like a breath of fresh air
and then
you took my breath away.

it's ironic how the people
we can breathe easy around
are the same ones
who make us forget
we need to breathe at all.

in no rush

i am learning you slowly.
i am taking my time here.

that is not to say that curiosity
isn't a fire within me.
(because it is.)
(because you are.)

but rather, that i am in no rush.
that i think i will
stay here for a while.

simplicity

how do i explain that my heart is, more often than not, swept into an elaborate dream? and yet, every time i'm with you, i somehow forget the big picture of us. i seem to do nothing but get lost in all the little details of who you are.

the little things have always been the loudest.
a smile. a touch. a word. a thought. a glance.
a prayer. a poem.

i try to write beautiful things about you but i am almost certain you've written them for me. it's like trying to take the oceans out of your eyes, or the sunrise out of your smile.

i tried telling you last night how i tuck memories of you in the backs of my eyelids as i fall asleep. it is because if i am to be swept into another elaborate dream, i know none better than the simplicity of this one.

none better than us.

there is no sweeter feeling
than thinking
i was dreaming about you
only to find

i was remembering.

rabbit hole

today the anxiety was a quiet presence. my hands shook (just a little) and it was harder to smile (just a little) but not because i wasn't happy. everything just felt deeply out of place like the frustration of walking into a familiar room where things look different, but you can't figure out what's changed. it is hard to explain, 'nothing is wrong, it's just hard to focus when my thoughts keep slipping down some kind of rabbit hole' or, 'i'm not in pain, there's just an odd feeling in the pit of my stomach that's very hard to ignore'. today the anxiety trod with quiet footsteps, but it still managed to walk all over me.

out of place

i am telling you, anxiety is always feeling like
something is out of place, and when you
can't find what it is, you start to think it's

you.

fine line

there is a fine line between
knowing you are flawed and
feeling like you are faulty.

lost amongst the clutter

somewhere amongst the clutter, you lost the envelope for the card i gave you on your graduation day. you didn't seem phased. told me that eventually you might throw out the card anyway. 'i'm not one to keep things,' you said, and my heart fell to the floor because who's to say you won't do the same with me?

i know it might sound stupid but i've dated the envelopes for everything i've written you and kept all our champagne corks because i'd like to believe we are building something together. like we are working towards a future. it only took a moment for that belief to tumble down.

i know this is an important time in your life and you have a lot of decisions to make but it's hard to hear you say you need to sort out your priorities. what i mean is, it's hard to hear you talk about whether you still want to play guitar or talk about your plans to save money. i sit there wondering if i will get to hear my name uttered somewhere in your list of priorities, or if i am just something else lost amongst the clutter.

with the money, you say you will buy a new car and tell me that i should buy a new phone. i tell you that i don't mind things that are a little broken and the fact that you don't agree worries me a little more than it should.

i'm so terribly sorry that i let us fall apart over a bunch of metaphors but my biggest fear is of being with someone who isn't afraid to lose me. i'm so scared of getting my heart broken that i'd rather break my own.

i know my anxiety often got the better of me and it ruined a couple of nights together, but it ruined more than a couple when i was alone.

you kept saying that you didn't know what to do to reassure me that you cared about what happened between us. i didn't know either and it sounds selfish, but i needed you to be the one to figure it out. you didn't know what to do for months that i was slipping away with my fears and all i needed was for you to do something (anything) to fight for me to stay.

a confession

i didn't water the flowers i got for my birthday. even when i knew i needed to. i just sat and watched them droop. tell me, w*hat kind of girl does that make me?* i wrote a poem about us in past tense even though we are still together. i just sat and wrote out goodbyes. tell me, *what kind of girl does that make me?*

i always let the things i love the most die. some nights, just a single thought is a shovel and i use it to dig my own grave. i am trying my hardest to not let you be the one i bury but even still, i come away with dirt on my hands and poems that look like obituaries for the funeral of us.

i swear i haven't lost my mind. it's just that i've lost you in my mind a thousand times over. and i guess i'm tired of changing out of colours appropriate for mourning, only to change back into them. i confess, i think about leaving you but there is not an ounce of me that wants to. tell me,

what kind of girl does that make me?

letting myself

i need you to know
that loving you
has always been
the easy bit.

it's letting myself
that is hard.

honey

i can tell you the day was sweet
but this would mean nothing.

there is fog in my lungs and i am
choking on the best way to tell you.
i breathe in uncertainty and try
to exhale something other than doubt.

every day i swallow something sharp.
(it does not matter what we call it.)

nothing goes down easy and
nothing stays down without a fight.

i can tell you the day was sweet
but what if i told you the truth?

that even sweet things go down
slow and *heavy*.

even honey scratches my throat.

re-read

i didn't write the book on anxiety but i have read it. once. twice. a couple of thousand times if i'm honest. i have dog-eared so many doubts so that i can revisit them at 3am. i have scribbled so many regrets in the margins. in pen, of course – so they are impossible to erase. i didn't write the book on anxiety but the pages are getting so worn. so am i. i keep wearing the same fears out and sometimes, it's just so tiring. to keep reading the book on anxiety. and feeling like you can't write the end.

soft torture

last night i had a dream i couldn't remember. it seems like every day i wake up with a head full of things to tell you but i can never think of what they are. the truth is, there has been this intangible thing moving inside of me for a while now. like something dislodged that i have spent far too many hours trying to shove back into place. i can't sit still when i'm with you and try as i may to brush it off, i can't shake the feeling that time is running out. that there are things still left to tell you.

i once sat on a train where a couple was breaking up – hungover screams echoing through the carriage. 'my love for you is like a snowball,' he said. she just laughed it off, thought it was the alcohol talking. but i smiled because i knew: love starts as something small. something that dislodges but then keeps moving inside of me, growing and growing as if it were a lump in my throat i can't clear.

i know it hurts sometimes – all the collateral damage i've made trying to fix things that don't need fixing. and how i came hairline close to breaking up with you. 'i'm scared,' you said, but my word, i was terrified. will i ever know what to do with this untouchable thing inside me? *i love you i love you i love you* and what the hell do i make of that? why would God give all this love for you to a girl like me who has dreams she can't remember and starts fires from candle flames?

i spend so much time trying to shift the weight of this snowball, letting it run its course down every side of the mountain you have become. you call me your tumblebug and it makes me smile because i know i make a mess. sometimes i kiss you because i want to say something but i don't know what it is. i don't know what it is and it hurts sometimes, you know?

it is so damn frustrating that it makes me want to throw my hands up, throw the towel in, start a fire from a candle flame, kiss you crazy, let myself become the thing that snowballs. and i know i sound insane but i think maybe that's what love is: the soft torture of having something so powerful moving inside of you and not having a clue where to put it.

tenants

i don't know how to tell you
that i am happiest when i am falling apart.
that if anger came banging on my door,
i would let it in.
that if sadness came pouring like rain,
i would open the windows.
i would let almost every emotion become
a tenant in the home that is my heart.

and even when they bicker endlessly
(even when the floors and ceilings
look like losing battles),
i would still let them stay.

because at least i have fought for something.
at least i am becoming someone.

even when they've made a mess,
at least they've made something out of me.

felt

you are such a soft soul
but i feel you
as something sharp around the edges.
as something more defined
than a camera could ever capture.

you flood my thoughts
like a disaster
that leaves no wreckage behind.
that leaves only happiness
as a quiet, gentle hum.

you are a new language
i cannot speak
because the words are stuck in my throat.
because you are felt in my bones.
and i think i would like you to stay.

dismantled

i'm always going to have this
insatiable need to turn the
alphabet into an artwork.

i'm always going to
lose you in the letters
along with my dreams and
fears and everything else
you're caught up in
amongst the mess that
is my mind.

but i guess if i were to
spell it out for you
slowly and simply,
if i were to dismantle it all
into a single sentence,
it would go something like:

i have more love for you
than i know what to do with
and i'd be so grateful if you
didn't break my heart.

the sentence in the silence

this is not a confession.
(at least, not an elaborate one.)

this is not a love letter.
(at least, not one that i will seal
and slip into your back pocket.)

this is nothing more than turning
silence into a sentence.

from the beginning, i have been
saying it. i have said it every time
soft skin empties itself into
calloused hands and yet,
some part of me fills.

i have said it and said it
but i will say it again:
i think i would like you to stay.

still

at the end of the day
i am both little girl
and aged woman.
both vivid imagination
and sepia pictures.

i tuck both memories
and dreams under my pillow,
forgetting which is which.

oh, how easily we lose track
of time. and how quickly the
present becomes the past.

and yet here i am, still
eyes fluttering
and mind flickering, still
heavy and light, still
feeling like every day with you
is one i want to remember.

how i will remember

i stopped taking photos and started taking feelings. if a place offered me happiness, i accepted it gratefully. if it offered nothing but a biting sadness, i still took it and kept it in the stores of my mind. ask me to remember something and i won't recall its fundamental elements of shape and light; i will remember how it made me feel. i started doing this with people too. if you are ever taken away by death or distance, i won't remember your exact features or the distinct sound of your voice. i will remember what i feel right now – how i feel like you are the best thing that has ever happened to me.

we never really grow up

your eyes are wide like you're seeing magic
for the first time. (how i start to look at you.)

the sky bursts into a sunset before us
and it looks like a cloud of dust
from opened cheese ball packets.
i think it's funny how even something as old as the sky
doesn't want to be an adult sometimes.

you hold my hand differently when we cross roads.
it's the 'i'm walking you safely to school' handhold
and i giggle because we are still learning –
not how to be adults but how to be children.
(how to colour outside the lines.)

you kiss me behind backs.
just a peck on the cheek.
the nose. the forehead.
like we are kids in the school playground.

we never really grow up, do we?
just grow older.

just run into the arms of different heroes.
(mine looks an awful lot like you.)

an afternoon with you

the light is honey and the air is sticky and
your presence makes the day feel sweet.

i feel safe around you.
a different kind of safe. like all the terrible
thoughts that kept me up at night and
all the things i worried about in the morning
have suddenly lost their weight.

weightless. that's how it feels.
to have you in front of me. to have someone
i can see and touch and love.

you feel like summer. you feel like the space
between christmas and new year's.
good things have been. good things are coming.
good things are right in front of me now.

everything i've been trying to say

i need to start by telling you i love you. i will dress my mind up in metaphors because that is how i have learnt to explain myself, but if it all gets lost in translation, know this: i really do love you. despite what i am about to say.

do you remember when you first asked me to be your girlfriend? you said that you planned to be there for all of me. not just the bits that you like. i never forgot that. and apparently, neither did you. because a short while into dating, when i told you about the anxiety that had taken up residence inside me, you said it again. you were here for all of me. not just the bits that you like.

you were there and you are here. you are here and it is wonderful, but sometimes it feels as though you've already left. it is not you. believe me, it is not you. but it is not me either. i have not yet decided whether to pen myself as victim or perpetrator but lately i've been thinking that i should stop carrying my flaws like crimes. as though i am not simply human.

i need to tell you about this anxiety that follows me. i know you don't see it when you walk with me, but it tugs at the hem of my dress. unpicks a stitch. then another. then another. i do my best not to let everything unravel. i try to clothe my vulnerabilities by tucking them into sleeves and pockets but sometimes it gets too hard to carry.

you often ask me why i don't tell you when i'm struggling. i guess i don't want it to weigh you down. i don't want it to sit as this burden between us. even though it does. i know i haven't always been the best at handling it. i go quiet in the car ride home. i crack the window open, just because i need fresh air or a glimpse of the moon or anything to feel like i'm not suffocating. anything to settle the chaos in my lungs.

it's true, i question us a lot. but it's not what you think. i don't question if i want this; i question if i'm wanted. but when my mind is foggy, i end up walking both paths. the world becomes a shopping centre on christmas eve where everything that is meant to bring joy turns into a blur of panicked voices. and i can't tell which one is mine. when worry overwhelms, all i hear is, 'i don't belong. i don't belong. i don't belong.'

i need you to know that i fight for you. please know that i go against my natural instincts. they say when adrenaline courses through us, we choose between 'fight' and 'flight' responses, and i am doing my best to fight. despite packing and unpacking suitcases in my mind, i am still here. i am still so happy to be with you.

when you asked me to be your girlfriend, i didn't know if i was good enough to hold us together. i wrote a list of all my imperfections but i never gave it to you. i read it back the other day, almost in disbelief at how none of it would have mattered to you. you have been here for all of me. not just the bits you like.

i know you feel like you don't know how to help. but i know that if i were to ask for it, you'd be here in a heartbeat. i need you to know that you're my hero. you're my hero and you're here and i'm here and it does not matter if we are good enough. because it was grace that brought us together. and i know it is grace that will keep us there.

the truth about belonging

sunday train journey

something about the plants that sprout
on train tracks moves me.
or the ocean from a city bridge.
i think it has something to do with
being where you're meant to be
but still not feeling like you belong.

sometimes i like to go to new places.
try them on like clothes to see if they fit.
most of the time, i leave with sore feet
and a tired heart because i know
(i know)

i am the one that doesn't fit.

poetry at the bus station

we are all moved by this weather.
by now, all the leaves are gone
and we are left with the
bare bones of ourselves.
the rain is relentless.
people step off the bus
with jackets pulled tight,
heads bowed and feet scrambling
for some place dry.

i can't help but watch them.
we are such a hurried people.
never lingering. always in a rush.
i'd be lying if i said i didn't feel
like i'm falling behind.
i'd be lying if i said i didn't feel the
slightest bit jealous. these people –
they all have some place to be.
when will i know where that
place is for me?

telephone wires

there is a deep sorrow
that hums in me like
telephone wires and
i want to tell you about it
but i can't find the words.

i think i am losing connection.

free-falling

i'm amongst all my favourite people,
a familiar face in a crowded room.
my mind wanders. my eye wanders.
it rests on a lone helium balloon.

we're both longing to reach for the sky,
we're both somewhere we don't really belong.
i know it's time to cut my ties –
move along, it whispers, *move along*.

i was asked why the sight of a balloon
could convince me to finally let go
but we are both made up this way –
up is the only direction we know.

one day we'll be anywhere but here,
one day we'll crash-land out of the sky.
but i'd much rather risk free-falling
than not knowing what it feels like to fly.

vagabonds

there's a strange beauty in the fragments of nature. the independent wanderers. an ember blowing from a fire. leaves falling from a tree and dancing through the air. shells washing up on a foreign beach, abandoning the ocean. raindrops falling from the sky. there's beauty in the way they leave the familiar to explore, to be free. if only we could be that brave. whilst their journey is over quickly, it's a moment of awe, mesmerising to watch. they are vagabonds. if these vagabonds could talk, i don't think they'd regret their leap of faith. for wherever they choose to land, they have greater purpose. they are renewed. the ashes, the compost, the sand, the lakes. even then they won't stay where they are. they roam the earth still, filled with experience, each place learning something new. they may not have a permanent home like their brothers who never left. they might never come back once they let go. but at least they are free. at least they are free.

fibre

i am unhappy and i wallow in it.

let my dress gather water stains
around the edges from all the
puddles i've stayed sitting in.

i wring the water from it and
hope that this sadness is
something in the fabric
not the fibre.

(something that will come out over time.)

see, there is something to be said about
sorrow. how in the grand scheme of things,
today's sadness only makes for a stronger
tomorrow.

see, it is always said that things happen
for a reason. but sometimes the meaning
of a moment cannot be traced so easily.

see, the earth swallows its own tears.
the rain seeps back into the soil.

see, everything that has been lost
will return in time.

and if this teaches you nothing else,
just know that your being human is

anything but wasted.

heavy

you feel heavy because you are
carrying the weight of the earth
inside of you instead of simply
being part of it.

the economics of letting go

lately i've been thinking about
physical things and emotional things:
everything i have to carry.
i feel burdened with memories.
and the way i will hold on to
an item or thought
just in case
it will be of significance later.

i rehearse lines from a conversation had.
memorise.
i never let anything gather dust.
because we never know if things
are going to be of
more or less
value in the future.

but lately i have stopped agonising over
the economics of letting go.
i am telling myself
it is okay to forget.
i am making room for better things.
like light.
like nothing at all.

finish line

when i was little, i used to watch raindrops sliding down the car window. i thought that perhaps they were racing to get across the finish line. i noticed the way the idle droplets were rescued by their brothers colliding into them and propelling them forward.

now that i'm older, i watch people. and i wonder why we are all still pretending that we don't need others to nudge us to keep moving forward when we get a little stuck along this journey we call life.

homesick

they warn us to not make homes out of people.
they say it will hurt too much while they're gone.
but what are these beating hearts good for
if not to be a place for others to belong?

my heart is a home with many rooms
with empty spaces for people to stay,
and sometimes we are lucky and find ones
who remain with us even when they are away.

i'm forever making homes out of people,
scattering bits of myself in the ones i trust.
and yes, it's messy but trust me it's better
than keeping them to myself to collect dust.

there are parts of others you need to take care of
and parts of yourself you need to give,
and while missing people is like being homesick,
i think this is how we are meant to live.

because we all have certain people
that for some reason feel like the safety of home.
it's true that without them you might feel lonely
but at least you are not doing life alone.

human

what do you want to do with your life? you ask.

i shuffle my feet uncomfortably and clumsily fumble around in my pockets, as though searching my vocabulary for a word that fits that description.

but there isn't really a job title that encompasses the scope of dreams i woke up with. i can't hand you tidy thoughts because my mind is a mess and i've spent the better part of daylight lazily swirling and swirling the paint palette of my plans until there is no telling which is which.

i think my eyes are coloured-in brown just to tell you this story of how i tried to make my life art but accidentally became it instead.

if you look closely, you can see flecks of blue i stole from the ocean when i first fell in love with freedom. but in the same exhale you'll find shifting shades of apricot and pebble pathways and every other kaleidoscope of home.

i'm not sure how to verbalise that i want to find one hand to hold every morning and watch as their voice softens my insides yet sharpens the edges of clouds so that i'm reminded to carry them in the safe space between being awake and dreaming. (it is where i live after all.)

i have not yet found the words to explain that i want to sing with the seasons: to know the ballad of winter by heart but never stop humming the victory cry of summer so that i can always be sure of its return.

i am afraid there is no category for the hearts like this: the ones that want very little but *want* and *want* and *want*. i fear you won't understand how the wanting doesn't make us empty, how the wanting is the oxygen that keeps our lungs full.

so i remove my hands from my pockets in defeat and tell you that i haven't figured it out yet. but the truth is, i don't need to figure out how to be anything more than human.

utterly and extraordinarily and miraculously human.

i want you to know
that i am trying to
make the most out
of the person i am

in this skin.

who am i?

i am always caught in-between.
between the urge to hide
and the wanting to be seen.

between the excitement of uncertainty
and the safety of absolutes.
between the yearning for freedom
and the idea of having roots.

i am an ever-shifting ocean
pulled back and forth between the tide.
a forever-swinging pendulum,
not still for long enough to decide.

not yet taken

i am tired of life being
measured in the steps
we have not yet taken.

i am tired of the way
we define ourselves
by where we are going.

as though right now,
this air,
these breaths,
are not already
extraordinary enough.

trying mornings on for size

maybe one day i'll wake up and things will be different. i'll know exactly who i want to be. but for now, i don't know how to stop trying mornings on for size. some mornings, i want to be all light and grace and wake up to watch the sunrise. others, i want to drown myself in melancholy and write until time forces me to stop. some mornings, i want to be freshly squeezed orange juice and big smiles and good vibes. others, i want to be searing hot coffee and blasting music and conquering the world before 6am. all i know is that i am twenty years old and i don't know what i want to be in the future because i barely know what i want to be today. but i thank God for new mornings and fresh starts and the freedom to be flawed and human. maybe one day i'll wake up and things will be different. but honestly, i hope that day never comes.

never let go

isn't life such a funny thing?

at any given moment, we could
get everything we've wanted,
or have it all taken away.

at any second in time, we could
make the best decision of our lives
or the worst.

don't you think life is the most
fragile and frightening thing?

doesn't it make you want to
hold on with both hands and
never let go?

untainted

sometimes what hurts more is the
could haves.
should haves.
would haves.

isn't it sad that pain is
more past than present,
but isn't it beautiful that
your next breath is untainted –
a chance you *could* and *should* take.

oh, if only you *would*.

like a child

sometimes my mind is like a child with a bad habit of wandering off. it is quite exhausting to take care of. it is too restless to let me sleep properly. it tosses and turns and taps me on the shoulder to let me know what it has been dreaming of. i admit that i am guilty of telling it grow up.

but it still searches for the good like a child trying to find fairies under fungi. it still paints a picture of a better world like a child drawing a broken family holding hands. it still has a sense of wonder like a child looking up in awe at the changing colours of the sky.

every day it reminds me that the world is a beautiful place.

it is a wild, hopeful, messy thing that i will spend my life chasing after, but how could i not want it? how could i ever wish this magic to be anyone's responsibility but mine?

thought collector

mostly i drift through days, collecting more thoughts than i can keep. i gather them up greedily, like treasures scooped up in my arms and spilling out the sides.

i have more than a handful, more than a head full of things to tell you:

(a) these city streets have become monochromatic but among the throngs of black, there is a girl in bright yellow shoes.

(b) i think she wore them on purpose, like an endless summer that refuses to be defeated by turning calendar pages. i think she is trying to tell us something.

(c) one day i want to drive a bright yellow car. they remind me of games we used to play on the school bus, and how beautiful it is to unknowingly make a child giggle, even for just a passing second.

there are letters inside letters inside letters that are trailing behind me and mostly, i don't know what to do with myself.

tell me, what would you do with a thought collector that is made of one heart and two hands and a million things i will never stop trying to hold?

dream collector

i hope you know that from dawn to dusk, i am collecting more dreams than my heart can remember.

i hope you know that when i say this, i mean that for me, the world fades in the blink of an eye, in the space of an exhale. but there are people, there are places, that remain in my mind in the full spectrum of light and colour:

(a) wisteria draped over white picket fences.

(b) grass in my hair and my little sister's heart beating next to me.

(c) sunlight i've swallowed and feelings i've followed. it makes more sense this way.

i hope you know the reason why i will always dream my way through the darkness. it is because the world is incredibly fractured, but oh, it has some beautiful pieces.

and i hope you know that i will spend my days picking them up. and i will spend my nights holding them together.

tangible

when i dream,
in a way,
i am already there.

cocoon

most days i tuck myself into
tangled thoughts.
i spin myself into a cocoon
that i do not emerge from for
quite some time.

it could be minutes, hours, days.
there is no telling.
some thoughts need time to process.
it is a transformation.
a metamorphosis.

i used to see it as my greatest weakness.
this feeling.
this loud silence.
this ravelling and unravelling.
but now i realise
it is also my greatest strength.

because while i am asleep to the world,
i am able to dream.
even if it is only fleeting.
even if i will eventually flutter awake.

what i mean to say is:
these days, i no longer wish for wings
and perhaps,
i am wiser for it.

i write this to you on
a bad day. it feels like part
of me hasn't woken up. like a
butterfly who prefers the cocoon.
i try to focus on what is real –
the pedestrian light is green
but i can't put one foot
in front of the other.
everything resembles a bad
dream. you tell me about silver
linings but the sound is drowned
out by a thunderstorm. you
want to know what the
worst part of me is?

my imagination.

i write this to you on
a good day. the wind feels
warm and i am touched by all
the tender things – the laughter in
someone's voice or the shadow
of the afternoon sun. the
world is a theatre and i
play the part of the
dreamer. i take whatever
contortion the clouds have
given us and shape them into
something beautiful. you
want to know what the
best part of me is?

my imagination.

mouth wide open

i am proud of my heart
and the way it has
learned to wake up
bursting and full
and still go out into the world
mouth wide open
and hungry.

monday morning

i wake up knowing i'm going to be okay, because no matter how complex my problems may get, i can always have simple joys. i can always have flowers and coffee and music. i wake up not exactly sure where i'm going this week, but on whatever path i may take, i promise myself that i will stop and smell the roses. i will appreciate the beautiful moments in this life and celebrate the good that is hiding in plain sight. i have seen that it is the thankful hearts that are the most generous, therefore i will make gratitude my goal, because i don't know much about how to change the world, but i am certain that the first step is to fall in love with it.

the fight behind my words

i try to make things beautiful but pain isn't always poetic, and my mind isn't always a metaphor. nonetheless, i will keep fighting to make my thoughts fit onto lined pages, not because i wish to confine them, but rather to set them free.

i admit, i am far too idealistic but i will continue this relentless pursuit of beauty because i refuse to accept this black and white world. that is perhaps why i hold to the view that life is art, because it is often the mundane experiences that are overlooked and the worst ones that we try to forget.

but i will continue to write about them, passionately assigning them meaning because in the end, they shape us just as much as the ones that can be photographed.

the world has many truths. i have found some and will continue to search for more. i will always try to capture their essence with an ink footprint. and yes, sometimes my words may fail to keep up but i will never ever give them up.

miracles

i know right now you feel broken
like a pile of shattered glass.
as though your wishes are all strewn
like dandelion seeds in the grass.

i know you feel like a snowflake
tumbling wildly on its fall.
you had hoped for a soft landing
but you're still swept up in it all.

bur your dreams aren't birthday candles
that you have one chance to blow.
and failure isn't permanent –
it just gives you room to grow.

the earth has its tragedies too,
but it's still a beautiful place.
just look at all the miracles
staring you right in the face:

broken windows can be repaired.
brand new dandelions can sprout.
and flames can be reignited
even when you blow them out.

it's the world's way of telling you
you're going to be just fine.
all you have to do
is give it a bit of time.

love letters

mondays are for fresh starts. for writing love letters to God. for thanking Him for forgiving me. for trying to forgive myself. things change when you wake up on the right side of forever. you don't worry so much about the little things. but you wonder and wonder about the little things too. like how fresh air can calm a troubled heart. or how this morning, i wrote to God in a love letter and this evening, He wrote back in a sunset. it looked a lot like love. it looked a lot like forgiveness. it looked a lot like a promise that i don't have to try so hard. because if He can make monday into a miracle, then imagine what He'll do with me.

mercy

i think we make mistakes but
they don't stay mistakes.

notice how we can make
a million wrong turns but still
end up on the right path?

i know i believe in mercy because
i keep creating messes and
He keeps transforming them
into miracles.

no sweeter sound

it's an answer so simple
yet so extraordinary.
all of my thoughts can be
silenced with one word.

every doubt, regret, failure.
every 'i don't know',
'i'm sorry', 'what if'.

every 'i've got this'
and 'i need help'
that exchange places
throughout each day.

but the loud noise
of traffic at such
intersections of thought
quieten with one word,
one answer – grace.

and i now know why
they call it a sweet sound.

you were the potter

and i was the clay.
complete in my design.
everything you made me to be.

you were the map.
guiding me through the world
i was placed in.
but i wandered so far away
that i lost myself
and everything you made me to be.

you were the composer.
angels sang lullabies when they
kept watch as i slept.
and oceans whispered melodies
of your greatness.
but i didn't listen for your
quiet songs of faithfulness.
i turned the volume up on tunes
that were the opposite
of everything you made me to be.

you were the author.
carefully and proudly writing my story.
but i was impatient and
smudged the blank pages with ink
declaring who i want to become,
not everything you made me to be.

"dear child,
I am still the potter
and you are still the clay.
I will remake you
into everything I made you to be."

poetry as a meeting place

sometimes when i share my poetry with people, i'm afraid i'm only showing one side of the story. there is no method to being a writer but very rarely do i write a poem using only one page. i love sharing my words but the truth is, sometimes it's hardly my work at all. what i'm trying to say is, there are two sides to every story and mine is the less well-known. mine is the back-of-the-page, behind-the-tapestry kind of side.

writing isn't a talent, it's just something God gave me when i needed it most – when He decided to turn my shaking hands into storyteller ones. and years later, you can still find me scribbling worries down as words until my handwriting doesn't look like the written equivalent of a stutter.

when i think about how God will use me, i don't have to wonder if i'm good enough. because i know i'm not. i'm always the one to bring the mess. even with an open heart and open hands, years later, this is still all i can offer.

but then there's the other side of the page. there's the turning of a new leaf. i think it looks something like grace. this is where we meet. day after day after day. in these pages. where i come to bury my brokenness and God comes to resurrect it into something beautiful.

this is why i believe. because most of the time, i'm nothing more than a tangled web of words. but God is the Steady Hand. the Soft Whisper. the Weaver. the Writer. the One who makes something worthy out of me.

faith

i can put a thousand questions
after "what if" and the answer
will always be faith.

forever

they say that seeing is believing
and so i say:

i see you in the sunsets that meet
the vast ocean and disappear
into the distance.

i see you in the never-ending
galaxies that i can only glimpse
with the naked eye.

i see you in the view of the
treetops or the city lights that
seem to stretch for an eternity.

even in this fleeting life,
i see you in all these wonders
that remind me to believe
there's such a thing as forever.

not there yet

before my fiancé and i started dating, he gave me a list of reasons he loved the sky so much. one of them stayed with me. he said that the sky is like a doorway. because the stars and the moon are always there, you just can't see them during the day. but when night falls, it is like a door opens and you have the chance to glimpse beyond.

sometimes my faith keeps me up at night. it paces back and forth down the empty hallways of my mind like a child up past their bedtime. too stubborn to sleep. (secretly, i do not want it to.)

some other secrets:

(1) sometimes i spend days with my hands in my pockets.
(2) i don't really know what to do with this body i am in.
(3) all love feels unrequited. even when it's not.
(4) i spend too much time in front of closed doors.

but then night falls. (something about the sky will always remind me of eternity.) and i take my hands out of my pockets. take a deep breath. try my best to love. even if clumsy. even if unrequited. (especially if unrequited.)

i open the door. greet faith in the hallway. it has always been trying to tell me something:

if nothing feels like home, it is because i am not there yet.

Afterword

At the start of writing this book, I compiled all the poems I have ever written. I went through all my old notebooks, the notes on my phone, study papers and loose receipts. I combed my house over the course of about three months. To this day, I am still finding more words in the margins of books I've read and stuffed in my bedside table drawer.

Looking back on all the pieces I'd written – some which I'm proud of, and many which I hope never see the light of day – I felt an overwhelming sense of doubt. I wondered, who am I to be writing a book? Do I even have anything to say?

I thank God for some kind words from others and incredible pieces of art that I clung to during this time. They were a constant reminder to not lose faith that God is writing a story in me and through me. While I might have liked to share a story that doesn't expose the most vulnerable parts of my heart to friends, family and strangers, I had to be faithful to God in sharing this one.

If I have said just one thing of importance in this book, let it be that you cannot find forever in fleeting things. I know. I have tried. It is terrifyingly obvious in these poems that I have longed to find a home in people and places on this earth.

Even though I now count myself incredibly lucky that I have found a sense of belonging in relationships and communities, I know that these too are temporary. I know I am not home yet.

There is a passage from the Bible in John 14:1-4 that I want to share with you. It says:

"Do not let your hearts be troubled. You believe in God; believe also in me. My Father's house has many rooms; if that were not so, would I have told you that I am going there to prepare a place for you? And if I go and prepare a place for you, I will come back and take you to be with me that you also may be where I am. You know the way to the place where I am going."

This passage almost moves me to tears when I read it. My Father's house in heaven not only has space for me, it has a place for me. It is not a fleeting home; it is a forever one.

This has changed everything about how I live.

It has given me the courage to love in a way that I could never have done by myself. I no longer need to worry about keeping my heart safe. I no longer need to fear that my efforts may be unrequited. Why should I? God has already given me enough love to last a lifetime; all I have to do is give it out.

Of course, I am still learning. I am still afraid most of the time. But knowing that this life is fleeting, I can start to let go of my need to find my place here, and love with the freedom of someone who knows that there is a place for me in my Father's home that can never be taken away.

Acknowledgments

To God, my Father – You planted the idea of this book in my heart as a seed. Then gave me everything I needed for it to grow. I dedicate this book to you.

To Sara Turnbull – Before these words were poems, they were experiences and feelings that you journeyed through with me. Having your support on my first draft was great, but your friendship over the years is what has been truly invaluable. Thank you.

To Aidan Kampers – Thank you for being the first person to read my draft cover to cover. Your feedback was of great help to me – I don't know what I would have done without your formatting suggestions. Thank you for offering your support on this project right from the beginning.

To Sarah Bennett – Thank you for reading through my manuscript in its later stages. Your feedback meant so much to me, as you understood and voiced exactly what I'd hoped to communicate in this collection. Thank you for your help in polishing some of the finer details.

To Susan Scott – I am so glad I had your help editing my manuscript. You were professional, thorough and kind. Thank you for your patience in answering my many questions. My book is better because of you.

To my Nan, Elsie – Thank you for sharing your love of words and butterflies with me.

To my family – I know at first you struggled to understand why I spent so much time with my head buried in a notebook. I want to thank you for giving me the space to pursue my passion for writing anyway.

To Matthew Huckel – For over three years, I've watched you work as a graphic designer to take people's dreams and carefully craft the details that make them real and beautiful. That is not only what you have done for me with this book, it is what you have done in my life. Thank you for all your hard work in creating my dream book cover, but most importantly, thank you for being my favourite dream.

Finally, I want to extend a heartfelt thank you to everyone who has encouraged me in this pursuit. It is no small feat to pour your heart out on paper, then attempt to gather it with enough grace that it can be produced into something resembling a book. Thank goodness I did not have to do it alone. Every small kind word felt big to me. I would not have had the courage or drive to put this book together if it were not for you.

From the Author

I want to thank you for reading this book.

As I set out to put my first poetry collection into the world, I did so with the intention to connect with other people. I believe words have a beautiful way of doing this. It is my hope that you have been able to find parts of yourself in these poems.

If you'd like to keep up with my writing, the two best ways are to (1) follow me on Instagram, and (2) sign up to my email list through my website.

Instagram | @rachelhuckel

Website | rachelhuckel.com

If you'd like to get in touch, please email rachelhuckel@gmail.com

I'd love to hear from you.

Gratefully,

Rachel

CPSIA information can be obtained
at www.ICGtesting.com
Printed in the USA
BVHW041154260522
638205BV00008B/271

9 780646 822013